THE WINNING EDGE

Tips for Creative Problem-Solving Teams

By Richard Safris

GOOD APPLE

Dedicated to:

**My team members who actually
wrote these rules:
Wade Beltramo, Jenna Dunbar, Rob Dunbar,
Jennifer Moriarity, Darcy Murphy, Mara Nagel, Mike Safris, Tracy Safris,
Steve Safris, Eric Shields, Jeff Stritmatter, Julie Waggoner**

**My co-coaches who helped refine and implement these guides to success:
Lynn Safris, Tom Dunbar, Darlene Dunbar**

And
**To my wife Lynn,
who cleaned up most of the messes, provided
fuel for thought
(brownies/animal crackers) and sacrificed
her time and space to the altar of
Creative Problem Solving**

Executive Editor: Jeri Cipriano

GOOD APPLE
An Imprint of Modern Curriculum
A Division of Simon & Schuster
299 Jefferson Road, P.O. Box 480
Parsippany, NJ 07054-0480

2 3 4 5 6 7 8 9   MAL   01 00 99 98 97 96

Contents

A Note From the Author

Most of the ideas in this book are drawn from experiences with middle and high school creative problem-solving teams, but the concepts will work for any team. These concepts are not earthshaking in their scope, but they may very well be the difference between simple success and outstanding success for your team. The ideas are drawn from my team's way of doing things, developed over years of being and working together. As a coach, I would never change something that worked for my team just because someone suggested something else, nor would I ever want anyone to totally pattern a team after what is in this book. Creative problem solving is a dynamic process. The success is in getting there, not in the arrival. What is presented here is simply one team's way of getting to their best solution.

As you go through these pages, be aware that the order is meaningless; what is important to one team will not be to another, and vice versa.

Every single page is a brainstorming exercise waiting to happen. If team members find a new concept or idea they like, their first step should be to brainstorm the uses or implementation of the concept or idea, thereby forever placing their own team stamp on its use.

Over the years, we occasionally compromised creativity to better prepare ourselves for competition. We tried to make practical use of our ideas in the real world situation of creative problem solving. However, we never sacrificed major creative thrusts to everyday limits. We simply recognized what the competition requirements were and exceeded them whenever possible.

Creative problem solving is not a life-or-death situation, but it can be either a pleasant or painful experience. I sincerely hope the ideas in these pages may reduce the pain and increase the gain for both coaches and team members.

RS

About the Author

Mr. Safris's teams have achieved second- and third-place finishes in international creative problem-solving competitions, with six other finishes in the top ten in international competition. His teams have won numerous awards for outstanding creativity at local, state, and national competitions. In 1994, Mr. Safris received the Spirit of O.M. Award at the Odyssey of the Mind International Competition in Ames, Iowa. This international award is presented annually to one individual for encouraging the development of cooperation, self-respect, appreciation, and understanding of others in the area of creative problem solving.

TIP #1

Have Fun

"Remember that happiness is a way of travel not a destination."
—*Roy M. Goodman*

"Happiness is a stock that doubles in a year."
—*Ira Colbleigh*

"Play is children's work."
—*Anonymous*

". . . Happiness keeps the wheels steadily turning,
truth and beauty can't."
—*Aldous Huxley*

Celebrate every chance you get—birthdays, good grades, major breakthroughs in the problem solving are all reasons for celebration. Celebrate especially if things aren't going well.

If you and your team are not having fun, there is something wrong. If a practice session seems to be going nowhere, talk about other things. In my experience, some of our best ideas came when we were off the subject.

Celebrate every chance you get—birthdays, good grades, major breakthroughs in the problem-solving are all reasons for celebration. Celebrate especially if things aren't going well.

Kids feel the pressure, too. Once in a while, set aside a Saturday or Sunday afternoon for a pizza party. It's a great way to sneak in a productive think session on the sly.

Creating a sense of team and togetherness is the best way to make problem-solving meetings happy and successful. This does not mean that every meeting needs to be a happy party. The happiness of overcoming shared difficulties is often the shortest road to shared success.

Failure is not an end, it is a new beginning. Failure is a springboard for new thoughts and creativity.

Learning to fail and not quit is perhaps the most valuable life skill that problem-solving competitions can teach!

Perhaps the most difficult problem that coaches face is dealing with bright children who have never failed before. Coaches must understand how much a first failure hurts. A coach must work hard to structure the practice sessions for success when failure rears its head during the process.

When dealing with failures prior to competition, teams must remember that they are dealing with a process, not the final goal. Failures are but one step of the process. Failure is not an end, it is a new beginning. Failure is a springboard for new thoughts and creativity.

Edison is supposed to have said, after numerous attempts to make a light bulb, that at least now he knew of several hundred ways not to make a light bulb. Each trial, no matter the outcome, gives us knowledge and narrows the problem.

TIP #2

You Only Truly Fail When You Fail to Try

"A minute's success pays the failure of years."
—*Robert Browning*

"There is the greatest practical benefit in making a few failures early in life."
—*Thomas Henry Huxley*

"The line between failure and success is so fine that we scarcely know when we pass it: So fine that we are often on the line and do not know it."
—*Elbert Hubbard*

Tip #3

Establish a Winning Position

"The key to success isn't much good until one discovers the right lock to insert it in."
—*Tehyi Hsieh*

"Nothing is more humiliating than to see idiots succeed in enterprises we have failed in."
—*Gustave Flaubert*

"Luck is a matter of preparation meeting preparation."
—*Oprah Winfrey*

In other words, all you can ensure, barring bad luck, is that your team is in the position to win.

Perhaps the most important concept of successful competition is that of establishing a winning position. Teams can work toward perfection in their performance, but perfection is nearly always unobtainable unless the competition is totally objective in nature. Judges are human and they will judge a performance based on an internal set of feelings, emotions, and values that you will never be able to identify before the competition.

Coaches do their team a great service by explaining that not everyone sees performances in the same way. That the team didn't score well doesn't mean that its performance was necessarily bad, but rather that the judges did not perceive the performance in the same way that the team did! In other words, all you can ensure, barring bad luck, is that your team is in the position to win.

First solutions are rarely the best solutions.

Always Break the Egg

In a Bill Moyers tape about Odyssey of the Mind, a problem-solving team is asked to make eggs stand on end by using various materials such as tape, paper, and craft sticks. The team simply tapped each egg on the table, breaking one end and making them stand on that end. Nowhere in the rules did it say that the egg couldn't be broken. "Break the egg" became our team's motto for the concept that creativity always comes first. These were among the last words spoken before every performance or competition.

Always emphasize the importance of creativity. We have always stressed that the top award at any competition would be the one for special creativity.

Teams must look beyond the obvious. Many times the materials themselves tend to lock teams into certain types of solutions. Often the solutions implied by the materials may cause teams to miss the simple or more creative solution.

There is creativity involved in reading between the lines of the problem. Top teams will often find a missing assumption that makes the problem considerably easier than it seems. Always remind the team that every word in a problem may have more than one definition. They must not stop at the first or most common definition. First solutions are rarely the best solutions.

"Less is more . . ,"
—*Robert Browning*

"The greatest truths are the simplest."
—*Julius and Augustus Hare*

"Our life is frittered away by detail . . . simplify, simplify."
—*Henry David Thoreau*

"The ability to simplify means to eliminate the unnecessary so that the necessary may speak."
Hans Hoffman

Tip #5

Clarify and Then Reclarify

"We are all, it seems, saving ourselves for the senior prom. But many of us forget that somewhere along the way we must learn to dance."
—*Alan Harrington*

"Nothing can be loved or hated unless it is first known."
—*Leonardo da Vinci*

"I keep six honest serving men, they taught me all I know: Their names are what, and why, and when, and how, and where, and who."
—*Rudyard Kipling*

Always try to use yes and no questions when inquiring about interpretations of rules so that there will be no confusion at competition.

Always write to the competition director for clarifications of any unclear rules or problems. If a question isn't answered, ask again. Always try to use yes and no questions when inquiring about interpretations of rules so that there will be no confusion at competition.

Also send drawings or photographs of questionable devices or constructions. Always save the responses received from state or national directors and have them with you at the competition. A staging area judge or worker can usually answer last-minute questions.

Do not take the competition site for granted. Write for a description of the availability of electricity (if needed), the type of floor, the presence of stairs, the width of doors, or answers to any other questions you feel might materially affect your team's ability to put on its best performance.

No team should ever assume unnecessary risk if the action generating the risk is not scored or will not materially affect the outcome of the competition.

If you don't take risks, you will very rarely win. I would suggest hanging in your work area a large poster with the following equation.

Risk = Reward

Every variable in a performance involves risk. By identifying and controlling variables in your performance, you can reduce your level of risk. Successful teams can controll variables in objective areas of scoring. Only the subjective areas of scoring should present major unknown risks for a well-prepared team.

Pushing the limits of creativity always carries an element of risk. Try to control the risks by carefully analyzing the rules and clarifying, where possible, any ideas that push the rules.

No team should ever assume unnecessary risk if the action generating the risk is not scored or will not materially affect the outcome of the competition. Study the scoring and concentrate your efforts on the areas that are scored, rather than an ill-defined categories such as "general impression."

Always make sure that the team knows exactly what is being scored. Effort in areas not scored may be laudable, but it will not affect the outcome of the competition.

TIP #6

Risk Is Directly Proportional to Reward

"Every advantage has its tax."
—*Ralph Waldo Emerson*

"A full cup must be carried carefully."
—*English proverb*

"Fruit is almost always found out on a limb."
—*American proverb*

TIP #7

If You Don't Know Where You're Going, You're Certain to Get There

"The means prepare the end, and the end is what the means have made it."
—*John Morley*

"It is not enough to be busy . . . the question is: What are we busy about?"
—*Henry David Thoreau*

Every meeting and practice should have a goal, preferably set at the end of the previous meeting.

Goal-setting is an absolute requirement. In most cases, team members will have to be taught the language of goal-setting. The coach can help structure the goals to make them attainable.

You must consider both performance and behavioral goals if your team is to be successful. The team should get in the habit of setting intermediate goals as stepping stones, while continually revising long-term goals as needed.

Every meeting and practice should have a goal, preferably set at the end of the previous meeting. We've posted goals on the ceilings of team members' rooms so that they look at and think about the goals every night before they go sleep. We regularly set goals in which everyone brings an idea to the next meeting aimed at solving some problem.

Always celebrate when you reach a major, intermediate, or final goal. Feeling good about attained goals is what makes harder goals more reachable!

Some early brainstorming sessions regarding acceptable behavior and methods of criticism and praise can be very effective.

I never require that my team members become friends. I do insist, however, that team members respect each other, both creatively and socially.

Teams must be taught to give and receive both positive criticism and praise. Unfortunately, nearly all children have learned that a smart remark or critical comment is emotionally safer than giving or receiving heartfelt praise or criticism.

Some early brainstorming sessions regarding acceptable behavior and methods of criticism and praise can be very effective. If you observe unacceptable behavior, stop and deal with the situation before it gets out of hand. For example, if you observe one team member criticizing another for being absent, stop what you are doing and brainstorm a solution to the problem of attendance. It is, after all, a problem-solving team.

Take the time to teach how to give and receive positive criticism, and the rewards will be significant.

TIP #8

Friendship Does Not Equal Respect

"Without feelings of respect, what is there to distinguish men from beasts?"
—*Confucius*

"True friendship is like sound health—the value of it is seldom known until it is lost."
—*Charles Caleb Colton*

"If you have respect for people as they are, you can be more effective in helping them to become better than they are."
John Gardner

TIP #9

Be Able to Quote the Rules Verbatim!

"It's them that take advantage that get advantage in this world."
—*George Eliot*

"You cannot put the same shoe on every foot."
—*Publilius Syrus*

"Laws are not masters but servants, and he rules them who obeys them."
—*Henry Ward Beecher*

Rules must always be read for what they do not say as well as what they say.

All teams must begin with the rules, for they are the foundation upon which the solution is built! All solutions built on shaky foundations will collapse at competition.

The coach and at least one team member need to be experts on the material included in the program handbook or the problem instructions. Just as the rules may penalize your team, they may also be used to protect it from incurring unnecessary penalties.

Rules change and new rules occur annually in every problem-solving program. As creative kids challenge the rules, new rules must be made to preserve the integrity of the contest. And as problem-solving teams become more sophisticated, so must the rules.

Rules must always be read for what they do not say as well as for what they say. Several sessions should be spent on reading, discussing, and interpreting the rules.

Practices should include backups for very important parts of the performance.

Always prepare an emergency plan for identified problem areas in your solution. Having a plan is not a lack of confidence; it is an acknowledgement of reality.

Practices should include backup plans for very important parts of the performance. Scored requirements, such as moving a flag from vehicle to vehicle during the problem, need a backup. These distraction activities, not directly tied to the actual solution, are often included in creative problems to separate the winners from the losers.

I always feel proud of teams that experience a disaster at competition, fix it as best they can, and continue with their solution. That is what competition and teamwork can and should be all about.

Teamwork requires that weaknesses be discussed and prepared for before they happen. While most adults see what can happen, kids often see only what they want to happen. In many cases, this is the difference between success and failure at competition.

TIP #10

Make Contingency Plans for Important Parts of the Performance

"Be prepared."
—*Boy Scouts manual*

"If something can go wrong, it will ."
—*Murphy's Law*

"And at the worst possible moment."
—*Corollary to Murphy's Law*

Details Equal Extra Points

"The tiniest hair casts a shadow."
– *Goethe*

"It has long been an axiom of mine that the little things are infinitely the most important."
—*Sir Arthur Conan Doyle*

"Inanimate objects are classified scientifically into three major categories—those that don't work, those that break down, and those that get lost."
—*Russell Baker*

Every movement and every word in a skit should have a motivation.

I had a team consider a dead fish to lend the smell of a fish market to a scene in having a skit. I had teams record live grocery-store music and elevator music so that their skits were just right. I had a team call the Egyptian Embassy to request a copy of the sheet music for the Egyptian national anthem. Then they digitized the music on a computer to be sure that they had it right. Details in a performance are important!

The rule is to elaborate in all things, since the first solution is almost always not the best solution. Every movement and every word in a skit should have a motivation. Check skits for sound, sight, smell, touch, taste (good or bad), lighting, movement, motivation, and anything else you can think of.

Observe the judges in early performances. What do they like and dislike? Watch their faces when things are done in those performances.

Always try to be unique.

Use visualization techniques during practice sessions to improve skill levels.

We have had good success with our teams doing visualization not only of the actual performance but also of specific problems. I firmly believe that until team members can visualize themselves doing each step of the performance correctly, they will not be able to do it correctly in real time.

Make the team believe that visualization works, and it will! Point out that what athletes do at the Olympics and what pro basketball players do before shooting a free throw are visualization techniques.

Use visualization techniques during practice sessions to improve skill levels, and then use them at competition as a relaxation technique.

TIP #12

Use Visualization as a Training and Relaxation Technique

"Where there is no vision, the people perish."
—*Proverbs 29:18*

"It isn't that they cannot see the solution. It is that they can't see the problem."
—*G. K. Chesterton*

"If you cannot dream it, you cannot do it."
—*Anonymous*

Tip #13

Do Not Give In to Superstition

"Superstition is the religion of feeble minds."
—*Edmund Burke*

"There is a superstition in avoiding superstition."
—*Francis Bacon*

"Superstition may be used as a fun pressure release valve but should never be allowed to become a substitute for reality."
—Richard Safris

Actually, I've had to deal with lucky geckos, socks, airplanes, shorts, underwear, trolls, shoes, stuffed animals, and jackets, among other things.

If having a lucky item or doing something in a certain way relieves the pressure, so be it. Let your conscience be your guide. If you don't like the word superstition, perhaps you could view it as a "precompetition routine."

I should point out that one team failed to find its lucky gecko and lucky airplane before a state meet and had a complete mechanical breakdown during competition. It was the only time that this team ever finished below second place at a state competition.

It is with a certain ambivalence that I speak of superstition. I believe that the individual coach must make the decision about how to deal with it. For my teams, focusing on something lucky was a way to relax prior to competition. For other teams, it might be divisive. It's an issue each coach must solve.

Sometimes, however, another team's performance can motivate your team.

Winning teams should believe that their destiny is largely in their hands, not in the hands of another team or coach. They should believe that if they do their best they will put themselves in that important winning position. A coach must constantly emphasize that the competition is between team members and their own abilities.

Sometimes, however, another team's performance can motivate your team. For example, one team of mine constantly talked about a team from Texas that had placed higher than they had at the previous year's world competition. My team constantly discussed this team's performance almost to the point of obsession. It became a benchmark and prime motivator for them.

TIP #14

We Have Met the Enemy and He Is Us

"Oh, I am heartily tired of hearing what Lee is going to do. Try to think what we are going to do ourselves."
—*Ulysses S. Grant*

"We lie loudest when we lie to ourselves."
—*Eric Hoffer*

"He was a self-made man who owed his lack of success to nobody."
—*Joseph Heller*

Predict Your Competition Score

"When schemes are laid in advance, it is surprising how often the circumstances fit in with them."
—*Sir William Osler*

"People see only what they are prepared to see."
—*Ralph Waldo Emerson*

"A danger foreseen is half avoided."
—*Thomas Fuller*

"Never underestimate self-fulfilling prophecy."
—*Richard Safris*

Team members should attempt to identify how many objective points they are going to get before the competition begins.

If you don't know where you are, it is impossible to lay out a path to where you want to go. Thus, part of knowing where you are, is knowing how many points you can depend on when competition starts.

Part of goal-setting should be an analysis of obtainable points. Team members should attempt to identify how many objective points they are going to get before the competition begins. This analysis of obtainable points will serve as a confidence-builder in strong performance areas as well as an analysis of weak ones.

In general, my teams have set goals that include all the objective points and 75% to 80 percent of the subjective points. Sometimes the team will identify objective points that it cannot attain. When this happens, the team must always forget about what it cannot get and concentrate on the areas in which it can get points.

Experienced team members will look at a problem and give a fairly accurate prediction as to what the top team score will be. Through practice they can determine where they stand and either polish their performance or make major changes to increase their opportunity to score additional points.

Taking creative risks is crucial; nevertheless, creativity must always be tempered with reality.

Creativity Must Be Valued Above All Else

Creative risk-taking should be the basic concept underlying all creative problem-solving competitions. If a coach constantly emphasizes creativity over performance, it will go a long way toward softening the blow of not winning at competition. Creative teams will always have a positive aspect to look back on when the competition is over, and usually a memento to hang on a wall. I am more proud of my team's Odyssey of the Mind World Ranatra (an award for special creativity) in spontaneous problem solving than I am of its second- and third-place finishes in world competition.

Taking creative risks is crucial; nevertheless, creativity must always be tempered with reality. Airplanes may soar beautifully but are useless without landing gear.

When selecting a creative problem-solving team, do not neglect kids whose behavior may seem inappropriate at first glance. A class clown might supply some very unique ideas. A very quiet student may be very quietly thinking of all kinds of creative solutions.

"There is a correlation between the creative and the screwball, so we must suffer the screwball gladly."
—*Kingman Brewster*

"Be brave enough to live life creatively. The creative is the place where no one else has ever been. You have to leave the city of your comfort and go into the wilderness of your intuition."
–*Alan Alda*

TIP #17

Have Forms Done Early and in Duplicate

"A little neglect may
breed great mischief . . .
For want of a nail the shoe is lost.
For want of a shoe the horse is
lost. For want of a horse
the rider is lost."
—*Benjamin Franklin*

"Measure a thousand times,
cut but once."
—*Turkish proverb*

"Better to be safe than sorry."
—*American proverb*

All clarifications or qualifying correspondence with authority needs to be duplicated and kept with the forms.

I personally have had the experience of finding out less than two hours before competition that all of the team's forms were 700 miles away on the kitchen table. I have also had the experience of watching kids do the forms the night before competition, when they might have been better off sleeping!

Forms should be viewed by the team as an opportunity to shine and gain advantage over other teams. Judges like well-written, neat forms.

All clarifications or qualifying correspondence with authority must be duplicated and kept with the forms. I suggest keeping the forms in a loose-leaf binder. Bills and receipts for all nonordinary purchases should be duplicated and kept with the forms as well.

Two complete sets of forms should be prepared and placed in the hands of two different team members to take to the competition. I have always made this the team's responsibility, and so far it has been a success.

Concentrate on the identified performance requirements and let "overall effect" take care of itself.

Successful teams should be certain that their performance description is accurate and clear. If allowed, a style form, script, or storyboard becomes a valuable vehicle for setting up your performance in the judge's mind.

Teams must remember that time is wasted on sets, props, and things that are not directly scored by the judges. Yes, these things are included in any "overall effect" category, but I suspect that most style judges base that score on an average of the other scores, or on the actual performance of the skit. Concentrate on the identified performance requirements and let overall effect take care of itself.

Make sure the team says what it means on the forms. There is a huge difference between scoring appearance, scoring method of presentation, and scoring the technology used in the presentation of something. If the team is not careful, the judges will end up scoring something the team had no intention of presenting. An example: On the stage a mechanical flower blooms in slow motion. If the form says, "Judge the flower," will the judges look at the flower's appearance, the mechanics of making it bloom, the presentation of the bloom, or whether or not the bloom is a flower or a weed? Always be precise in your descriptions.

TIP #18

Forms Must Say Exactly What They Mean

". . . If one has anything to say, it drops from him simply and directly, as a stone falls to the ground."
—*Henry David Thoreau*

"Proper words in proper places make the true definition of a style."
—*Jonathan Swift*

Coaches Are Facilitators, Not Directors

"A pig that has two owners is sure to die of hunger."
—*English proverb*

"Property is the fruit of labor, property is desirable; it's a positive good."
—*Abraham Lincoln*

"The highest law gives a thing to him who can use it."
—*Ralph Waldo Emerson*

"An ill favored thing, sir, but mine own."
—*William Shakespeare*

If teams feel that they own their solution, they will take pride in it and work hard to make it successful.

For teams to be successful, they need to have ownership of the process and the product. Every time the coach intrudes on this relationship between a team and its chosen solution, he or she chips away at the ownership of that solution. Winning coaches should provide the site, the food, and the social control, if necessary, and then get out of the way.

If teams feel that they own their solution, they will take pride in it and work hard to make it successful. Coaches may answer questions, but they must take care to answer them succinctly. I personally feel that a coach should answer the question, "Do you like that?" with a yes or a no, but nothing else. In fact, yes and no answers are almost always the safest way to answer questions.

To be a good coach or facilitator is a difficult job. Keeping your own ideas out of the mix when you are instinctively a teacher is a difficult matter, indeed.

Winning coaches will try to let their teams establish the ground rules of where and how they work best—since they are doing the actual work.

Whether at your home or in school, your team needs work space. Reserved space needs to be available so that a mess can be left if necessary. This does not mean that rules about getting tools out and putting them away cannot be enforced. It *does* mean that if everything has to be taken out and put away each time, you will literally waste a great portion of work time each meeting.

It is particularly valuable if you allow team members to work on some part of the problem by themselves when other team members are not present. You will be amazed at how much faster the work goes when one or two highly motivated team members just show up and do things on their own. My high school teams rarely managed more than one or two hours together a week, but team members often worked alone or in pairs throughout the week.

Identify your team's working style and try to accommodate it. Some members will work in a group, some with partners, and some alone. Some students work well late at night, others early in the morning. Winning coaches will try to let their teams establish the ground rules of where and how they work best— since they are doing the actual work.

TIP #20

Work Areas Must Be Freely Accessible

"Home is not where you live, but where they understand you."
—*Christian Morgenstern*

"The ornament of a house is the friends who frequent it."
—*Ralph Waldo Emerson*

"What one knows is, in youth, of little moment; they know enough who know how to learn."
—*Henry Adams*

Play to the Judges, but Never Ignore the Audience

"If you give audiences a chance, they'll do half your acting for you."
—*Katharine Hepburn*

"Every now and then, when you're on stage, you hear the best sound a player can hear. It's a sound you can't get in movies or in television. It is the sound of a wonderful deep silence that means you've hit them where they live."
—*Shelley Winters*

Eye contact is the best insurance that the judges will not miss something.

The judges, not the audience, are scoring the problem. Do not alter the performance just to accommodate the audience. If the team is doing something subtle or important in the scoring, a special effort to make eye contact with the nearest judge will help emphasize the event. Eye contact is the best insurance that the judges will not miss something. Use it all the time.

Words must be projected, since the judges can't score what they can't hear. However, there is a difference between projecting and yelling.

If your team has more than five members, the additional members might distribute handbills to the audience as a way for them to be involved. (Check the handbook for rules on handbills and check with the staging area judge or other authority to qualify this activity to avoid breaking some competition rule.) The use of handbills and advertising is an advantage that most teams ignore. Aggressive teams can increase their audience appreciation dramatically and thus increase the apparent audience reaction.

Audience participation is a plus for any performance. A happy, appreciative, vocal audience will affect the judging in a positive fashion.

**Enthusiastic, complete answers
will affect the score in a positive fashion.**

Teams should anticipate and practice questions that they feel the judges may ask about their solution. The more unique and creative a solution, the greater the chance of questions at the end of the performance. If a question is asked, it should be answered by the team member that did the work or had the idea. Enthusiastic, complete answers will affect the score in a positive fashion.

The whole area of entrance and exit at the competition site is often overlooked by creative problem-solving teams. I believe the demeanor and actions of a team entering and leaving a competition site truly affects the score that the team will receive. The affect may be subtle in the case of subjective scores, or even overt, in the shading of very close objective judgments.

TIP #22

Try to Anticipate Judges' Questions and Reactions

"However much thou art read in theory, if thou hast no practice, thou art ignorant."
—*Sa Di Gulistan*

"Practice is nine-tenths."
—*Ralph Waldo Emerson*

"I have a belief that kids who do wonderful things are usually more than happy to tell you how they accomplished it.
–*Richard Safris*

Murphy's Law Is a Reality

"Now and then there is a person who is so unlucky that he runs into accidents which started out to happen to somebody else."
—*Don Marquis*

"Fate is not an eagle, it creeps like a rat."
—*Elizabeth Bowen*

"Things never break when you're not using them."
—*Richard Safris*

There will always be three other school activities on competition day.

Murphy's Law states the following.

"If something can go wrong, it will go wrong, and at the worst possible moment."

Some corollaries of Murphy's Law are as follows.

- A dropped tool always rolls under the workbench.

- Paint always splashes on clean surfaces.

- There will always be three other school activities on competition day.

- You can always find three bolts and nuts when you need four.

- If all the nuts have 1/2-inch heads, the 1/2-inch wrench is the one that is missing.

- Need C batteries? The stores are closed and you have every other size.

- Need brown paint? All the colors of the rainbow are in your garage except brown.

Success at spontaneous problem solving (brainstorming) can be described in three words: practice, practice, practice.

In almost all competitions, the top five teams will be within ten points of each other after the objective points are counted. The style score, spontaneous score, or other subjective criteria will determine the champion.

In O.M., I have had teams finish all over the spectrum in long-term scoring, but no team has ever finished out of the top ten in spontaneous scoring or the top ten in style scoring. And only once has a team of mine finished out of the top ten in total score at world competition. Their success is not due to their strong long-term objective solutions, although for the most part they have been very competitive. They have succeeded because of their understanding of the subjective parts of the scoring, such as style and other opinion judgments.

Success at spontaneous problem solving (brainstorming) can be described in three words: practice, practice, practice. Brainstorming techniques improve with skill. Free association is a learned skill. Listening to and building on the ideas of others are learned skills. Have a brainstorming session at every practice.

TIP #24

Get in Position With Objective Points, Win With Subjective Points

"All life is 6 to 5 against."
—*Anonymous*

"Brainstorming ability is the cornerstone of success in nearly all creative problem-solving competitions."
—*Richard Safris*

TIP #25

Choose a Theme the Judges Will See Only Once During Competition

"The merit of originality is not novelty; it is sincerity."
—*Thomas Carlyle*

"Anybody who is any good is different from anybody else."
—*Felix Frankfurter*

Comedy is usually the safest route to the judges' hearts.

Our five highest-scoring themes were:

- Revising history from the point of view of hybrid corn plants.

- Intelligent mutant clams in search of their heritage.

- A vehicle with grocery carts and "food" characters.

- Super "veggie" heroes—fighting crimes against good nutrition.

- In a problem requiring something in "full glory," a plain burger turning into one with everything on it.

Here are recommendations for team members:

1. Avoid sexual, religious, and profane comments.
2. Remember that judges are adults with adult points of view. What is funny to you may not be to them.
3. Avoid game-show themes, Disney characters, MTV, and current movies. (Satire would be the exception to this rule.)
4. Comedy is usually the safest route to the judges' hearts. But a well-done dramatic piece will often stand out.

Teams must leave some room for error in the timing of the performance.

Performance solutions will be accomplished faster in competition than they are in practice. Barring some breakdown, everything speeds up. Kids will talk and respond faster than they do in practice. They'll need to work on slowing down or they may not be understood.

Teams must leave some room for error in the timing of the performance. We usually allow at least 20 seconds of slack time in our performances to allow for ad libs.

Write for clarifications or rules interpretations if the instructions are not clear about using a watch.

Visualization can help with timing. Cued visualization (where the coach verbally cues how far into the performance the team is while it is visualizing) can help timing.

Time can almost always be saved by starting the skit in one area while another area of the stage is still being set up by other team members.

Remember, if the performance needs to be shortened, cut from the things that have nothing to do with the scoring of the problem. Look at the scoring sheet!

TIP #26

Time Is the Enemy

"Time is a file that wears and makes no noise."
—*Anonymous*

"The butterfly counts not months but moments, and has time enough."
—*Rabindranath Tagore*

"Those who make the worst use of their time are the first to complain of its brevity."
—*Jean de La Bruyère*

Tip #27

Successful Teams Never Stop Talking

"Much unhappiness has come into the world because of … things left unsaid."
—*Fyodor Dostoyevski*

"Good, the more communicated, more abundant grows."
—*John Milton*

"The art of conversation is the art of hearing as well as being heard."
—*William Hazlitt*

"Think before you speak is criticism's motto; speak before you think is creation's."
—*E.M. Forster*

Nothing impresses judges more than a team's proper handling of far-out ideas.

The creativity of a group can be greatly enhanced by having team members simply talk about what they are doing, not necessarily to anyone, but to everyone. Free association is a powerful tool for creative problem solving.

During "problem solution," unless silence is mandatory, a thoughtful babble is desired. Kids can talk and listen at the same time. To hear and consider, reject or build on the expressed ideas of others is the heart of group problem solving.

When contestants are allowed to talk during competition, they must be taught not to speak in whispers but to talk loud enough for the whole team to hear an idea. Team members must learn not to react to bad ideas negatively but to reject them silently and try to offer better alternatives. Nothing impresses judges more than a team's proper handling of far-out ideas.

Good ideas should be drawn to the attention of the rest of the team for evaluation. Teach team members to be assertive without being aggressive. Team members must learn to pick out good ideas from other members and second them so that the whole team will pay attention.

Always read the problem for what it does not say.

Get rules clarified so that the team can see the problem solution clearly. In spontaneous problem solving, unless the rules specifically forbid your solution or it is obviously against the spirit of the problem, try it.

Problem-solving judges can be questioned. Use the opportunity to question the judges before time begins. Before beginning a nonverbal problem, ask the judges if they will respond to questions during the problem solution.

As I mentioned in Tip #4, breaking the egg is a good example of reading between the lines. Another example is turning a table on its side to use it in some special way. For example, in building a high tower, it might make sense to start building down from the ceiling to the table instead of going up from the table toward the ceiling.

Always read the problem for what it does not say. In spontaneous competitions, always assign one team member to quickly reread the problem. As other team members start working, the reader may pick up a special nuance that was not picked up in the first reading. If you are not pushing the rules, you are not pushing hard enough creatively.

T**IP** #28

Win by Reading Between the Problem's Lines

"The most subtle, the strongest and deepest supreme art is the one that does not at first allow itself to be recognized."
—*André Gide*

"Some people will never learn anything, for this reason, because they understand everything too soon."
—*Alexander Pope*

TIP #29

Teamwork Is the Essence

"We go right enough … If we go wrong together."
—*George Santayana*

"We must all hang together, or assuredly we shall all hang separately."
—*Benjamin Franklin*

True teamwork occurs only when each team member begins to understand how other team members will react to a situation.

A coach must constantly work to build a sense of team if successful problem solving is the goal. Team-building requires that the following concepts be understood.

- We all have our skills and our weaknesses.

- The words "Can I help?" are powerful.

- Don't criticize unless you can offer a viable alternative.

True teamwork occurs only when each team member begins to understand how other team members will react to a situation. If certain team members do not seem to be getting a handle on team relationships, the coach should take them aside and explain the cause and effect of what they do and say. A simple example can be the difference between a proper and an improper response to praise and criticism. Team-building is an ongoing activity, enhanced by celebration and shared difficulties.

Each team member should set individual goals or performance goals for what he or she is working on at each meeting.

The setting of attainable goals is a learned skill. If kids aren't given the chance to set their own goals and revise and analyze those goals for themselves, they will eventually figure out that they are working for the coach, not for themselves. Here is where a good coach will help, but not control; guide, but not direct.

The team should keep the long-term (usually completion-related goals) and intermediate goals in sight, but work on short-term goals, marking off these as they are reached. Each team member should set individual goals or performance goals for what he or she is working on at each meeting.

Goals should be posted in the work area. Teams might post the goals on bathroom doors, the refrigerator door, and on their individual locker doors at school. I guarantee that they will see them more often in those places than anywhere else.

TIP #30

Every Session Begins With Goal-Setting And Ends With Analysis

"The world stands aside to let anyone pass who knows where he is going."
—*David Starr Jordan*

"The secret of success is constancy to purpose."
—*Benjamin Disraeli*

Tip #31

Every Team Has a Personality Based on Its Members

"Be what you are. This is the first step toward becoming better than you are."
—*Julius Augustus*

"Rain beats the leopard's skin, but it does not wash out the spots."
—*Ashanti proverb*

Coaches should avoid choosing themes for their teams.

Every team must find its own personality and stay true to that personality if it is to succeed.

Several years ago one of our teams decided to try a serious theme instead of comical one. One night, someone asked if anyone was having fun. After some discussion the team members decided that the theme was just not right for them. The script, already partially written, was abandoned. The props, already constructed, were redone, and the team went for a new theme only weeks before the regional competition.

Coaches should avoid choosing themes for their teams. This outside assistance meddles with the creative process and will probably lead to trouble in the long run.

Coaches should watch carefully and determine in their own minds the team's personality and work habits. Coaches who impose their own work habits on their teams are doomed first to unhappiness and second to failure.

Use what team members have seen at the competitions or on tape as a springboard to new concepts and ideas.

If you can, attend a national or international problem-solving competition with your team.

I firmly believe that many teams repeatedly qualify as national or world finalists simply because of the experience of being there the first time. The experience of competing at that level is very exciting and motivating. But more important it is helpful to see all the different approaches to the solution of one simple problem. If you can't attend higher level competitions, find out if videotapes are available and watch them with your team.

Use what team members have seen at the competitions or on tape as a springboard to new concepts and ideas. By watching tapes or attending competitions, your team can get a feel for what is needed to win as well as gain many new ideas on how to do things.

Never underestimate the power of example. If team members are able to see other teams elaborating the solutions beautifully, either live or on tape, they may get the idea that they can improve their own solution.

TIP #32

Attend Higher Level Competitions as a Competitor or Observer

"You know more of a road by having traveled it than by all the conjectures and descriptions in the world."
—William Hazlitt

"He who neglects to drink of the spring of experience is likely to die of thirst in the desert of ignorance."
—Ling Po

Tip #33

The Performance Must Show Motivation for Every Action

"All that we do is done with an eye to something else."
—*Aristotle*

"However brilliant an action, it should not be esteemed great unless the result of a great motive."
—*François de La Rochefoucauld*

If the idea doesn't fit with the overall theme or concept, it must be abandoned, no matter how clever or cute.

Excellent performances blend into one smooth, seamless flow. Everything has a reason for happening. Props are moved for a reason. Speech is purposely connected to other speech. Players look at other players when they are speaking to them.

Sometimes, nonacting team members can hide from the scene by dressing in black. Players who wish to disappear during a scene can also do so by adopting a head down, motionless posture with their faces away from the audience.

Costume changes should take place out of the sight of the audience, when ever possible. I have seen high scores given to teams that have designed dual-purpose costumes that change by being turned inside out.

Teach the team to constantly ask "Why?" when different ideas are proposed for inclusion in a performance or skit. If the idea doesn't fit with the overall theme or concept, it must be abandoned, no matter how clever or cute.

A good ending will make your team's entire performance stand out from the rest.

The beginning grabs the attention of the judges and the audience. It will set the tone. It serves notice to the judges that it Is time to pay attention to this performance. It's going to be a good one!

The middle tells the story. This is where you get your message across or fulfill objective and subjective point requirements. Every movement and word must have a motivation and a result. The action must move smoothly and constantly. If a prop change must take place, the action should continue to one side.

The end is apparent to the audience and the judges. The team doesn't have to say "the end" or "we're done." The beginning and the middle have set the scene for the ending or climax of the performance.

The ending needs to leave the judges feeling good about the performance as they are filling in their score sheets. A good ending will make your team's entire performance stand out from the rest.

TIP #34

Skits Should Have an Identifiable Beginning, Middle, and End

"A good beginning makes a good ending."
—*English proverb*

"The unfinished is nothing."
—*Henri Amiel*

"A whole is that which has beginning, middle, and end."
—*Aristotle*

TIP #35

Always Have Questions to Ask in the Staging Area

"There aren't any embarrassing questions, just embarrassing answers."
—*Carl Rowan*

"To question a wise man is the beginning of wisdom."
—*German proverb*

"Better ask twice than lose your way once."
—*Danish proverb*

Be assertive in a friendly, professional style. Your attitude should be one of partnership

Has your team ever had a last-minute idea that stretched the rules? Perhaps you can get an informal clarification or rules interpretation during staging.

The staging area judge should be notified if some part of the performance is very subtle and subject to being missed or if handbills will be distributed. Explain any messes that will occur and how they will be cleaned up immediatley after competition.

People other than team members will probably be allowed to help remove the props after the performance, but it pays to check with the judges. Ask the judges to delineate the boundaries of the performance area if that seems be a problem.

Nothing should ever be left in the staging area! Many contests have penalties for failing to clear the staging area.

Be assertive in a friendly, professional way. Your attitude should be one of partnership with the judges. They are there to assist as well as to judge.

**To be successful, teams
must attempt to control all variables.**

If the contest allows prequalification of its rules, you must get prior approval for any segment of your performance that tests or stretches the rules of the competition. If you don't have a proprietary clarification or rules interpretation response in your folder at competition, you probably haven't pushed the rules hard enough to be a successful team.

Pushing the rules without attempting to clarify exactly what the rules are is an uncontrolled variable. To be successful, teams must attempt to control all variables. Certainly, you may not get a ruling in your favor, but that in itself may be instructive and is certainly a valuable piece of information to have before competition.

The team must always read the rules in search of subtle nuances and missing controls that might make the solution easier to identify than the writer intended. It is always helpful to refer to a dictionary for the various meanings of the words in the problem. You may find an amazing simplification because of definition, or you may open up new doorways to creativity by finding an unexpected definition of a key word in the problem.

TIP #36

Always Have at Least One Clarification in Your Folder

"Whoever starts out toward the unknown must consent to venture alone."
—André Gide

"Penetrating so many secrets, we cease to believe in the unknowable. But there it sits nevertheless, calmly licking its chops."
—H.L. Mencken

Understand That Work Never Divides Evenly

"Chop your own wood and
it will warm you twice."
—*Henry Ford*

"The only place where success
comes before work
is in the dictionary."
—*Vidal Sassoon*

"It is not upon thee to finish the
work; neither art thou free to
abstain from it."
—*The Talmud*

**Each team must have its own way of
handling the "fairness" issue.**

Perhaps one of the most stressful situations occurs when certain team members refuse to share in the labor needed for the solution. Each team must have its own way of handling the fairness issue. Following are some things to consider.

- Have we identified the skills of each team member and directed work into that area?

- Have we made an attempt to identify each team member's preferred work and work method (solitary, group, art, logical)?

- Do we offer positive criticism when the nonworker does produce?

Absenteeism can be a problem. The team should make sure there aren't legitimate reasons for the absence before casting stones at the offender. Offer rides, and work at making members more comfortable on the team. Let them do assigned tasks at home, away from the team, if necessary.

If divisive behavior becomes a problem with any team members, the coach may need to talk with the offender or the parents. If necessary, document the offense and the attempted remedies, and then sever the relationship cleanly and clearly.

**Experienced teams will study
the judges and their scoring histories.**

Experienced teams will study the judges and their scoring histories. Teams should understand that many judges remain in the same problem year after year. This is certainly true at national competitions and also may be true at many state meets.

Experienced teams may actually change things they think certain judges will mark down or fail to understand. I have listened to discussions in which team members decided to adjust parts of their performance for a state meet because they were not sure that certain state judges would understand the subtlety or the concept.

In my opinion, analysis of the judges and what has worked at past competitions is a very important part of the continued success of winning teams. Winning teams will debrief after every competition and discuss what worked and what did not work. Team members may even seek out the judges after competition and ask them why they liked or disliked a certain part of the performance. If this question is asked in a nonthreatening manner, valuable knowledge will be gained for future reference.

TIP #38

Know Who the Judges Are

"Happiness is composed of misfortunes avoided."
—*Alphonse Karr*

"Luck is the Residue of Design."
—*Branch Rickey*

"A windmill is eternally at work to accomplish one end, although it shifts with every variation of the weathercock and assumes ten different positions in a day."
—*Charles Caleb Colton*

Tip #39

Learn Relaxation Techniques

"The bow too tensely strung is easily broken."
—*Publitus Syrus*

"As a rule, what is out of sight disturbs men's minds more seriously than what they see.
—*Julius Caesar*

"We are more often frightened than hurt: Our troubles spring more often from fancy than from reality."
—*Seneca*

Sometimes the coach can take the pressure off of team members by giving then a diversion to consider.

I have always used relaxation techniques with students before and during competition. Kids are just as susceptible to tension and pressure as adults are. We have used relaxation techniques such as screaming our heads for a few minutes in a vacant area far from the competition. We have tried meditation techniques with varied results. We have always had good results with visualization.

Sometimes the coach can take the pressure off team members by giving them a diversion to consider. One coach wore lucky socks with ugly fish on them and chartreuse underwear. Another coach had "Good Luck" painted on his bald head and socks painted on his feet. These goofy things relieved some of the tension.

As coaches, we always try to convey an attitude of "whatever happens, we know that you will do your best."

**The team should have a plan
for the 24 hours preceding the competition.**

The team should have a plan for the 24 hours preceding the competition. The plan should include the following:

- Identification of individual team members' responsibilities for forms, costumes, music, props, prop loading.

- Times and places for prop loading, transportation to the competition, and an actual plan for the competition day itself.

The plan for competition day should include:

- A visit to the competition site before competition begins, preferably the first thing after arrival.

- Team activities during the day such as having lunch, visiting competitions, and making team preparations.

Team preparation time should not be stretched over the whole day, but rather be concentrated into a few hours. We always checked out all costumes, props, and forms upon arrival. Then we occupied our time in other ways until it was time to get ready for the competition. We always traveled as a team on competition day. We always emphasized that we were either going to win together or lose together—never apart.

Plan the Competition Day

"Fear comes from uncertainty."
—*Edgar Watson Howe*

"Better one safe way than a hundred on which you cannot reckon."
—*Aesop*

"We must ask where we are and whither we are tending."
Abraham Lincoln

"The mightiest rivers lose their force when split up into several streams."
—*Ovid*

TIP #41

Voting Is Almost Always Team-Destructive

Avoid dividing the team into two camps.

At times, all teams will come to loggerheads about something. Some kids have very strong personalities and are used to being right and leading others in the direction that they choose. I once asked one such team member, "What have you gained from creative problem solving this year?" He answered, "I have found out that occasionally other people have good ideas, too."

When you reach an impasse, try discussion or let the issue sit for a session. If that fails try a written matrix (see pages 79–82), using criteria set by the team to determine the worth of the idea. As a last resort, take a vote using a secret ballot. The coach should count the ballots. In the event of a tie, further discussion of the pluses and minuses of each idea should be tried.

In many problem solving competitions, the coach may not suggest ideas, since that would be "outside assistance." If an impasse arises, try parallel development of ideas until one or the other becomes the more obvious choice.

Avoid dividing the team into two camps. When some team members lose and others win, the team as a whole has lost something.

Let the chips fall where they may.

Many problem-solving competitions have more than one level of competition. That is, they move through district, regional, state, and possibly national contests. No matter what the level of competition, the coach must continually emphasize that the true competition is between the team and the material or the problem. The team cannot control the judges. Instead, the team must strive to control those things that are controllable.

No team should go to competition expecting victory over an opponent. Team members should be prepped by the coach to simply reach for their own full potential and let the chips fall where they may. They must realize that judges and sites differ from contest to contest. Indeed, a winner in one judge's mind may be a second-placer in another's.

Every contest is a new set of interpretations, likes, and dislikes by the judges. Always have your team prepare for its best performance, knowing that its best may, indeed, not be good enough for a particular set of judges.

TIP #42

Each Stage of Competition Stands on Its Own

"Nothing is so good as it seems beforehand."
–*George Eliot*

"The only way to predict the future is to have power to shape the future."
–*Hoffer*

"Yesterday is not ours to recover, but tomorrow is ours to win or to lose."
–*Lyndon B. Johnson*

TIP #43

Develop Self-Reliance

"Fate keeps on happening."
–Anita Loos

"Fate leads the willing and drags along the reluctant."
–Seneca

"I claim not to have controlled events, but confess plainly that events have controlled me."
–Abraham Lincoln

If you do the work for kids, they will never learn to do it for themselves.

One of my goals as a coach is to develop in team members self-reliance and self-esteem. If you continue to do the work for kids, they will most assuredly let you, and never learn to do it for themselves.

The costumes and props are the team's blood, sweat, and tears. My teams always took care of their own props. When they knew that I wasn't going to do it for them, they did a wonderful job themselves.

Once I had a team build a trailer. It was designed to hold a motorized vehicle for a trip from Des Moines, Iowa, to the University of Maryland. The team members designed the trailer so that it could be taken apart after arrival in Maryland and placed in a box that served as the cover of the trailer. The trailer was shipped home to Iowa after the competition. It worked beautifully!

Try not to load props and costumes onto a communal prop truck if you can help it. The team has plenty to do without having to repair props that have been damaged in transit.

Make sure that your team enters the competition site in a professional, competent, friendly manner.

Make sure that your team enters the competition site in a professional, competent, friendly manner—obviously a team ready to compete. At the upper levels of competition, this may be the winning edge. I have judged and I have watched teams enter areas while being harassed by their coach, dominated by one team member, or totally disorganized and arguing with each other. I know what my feelings were, and I won't deny them.

When a performance is over, the scoring may not be. Many judges may still be thinking about their scores. Attend to the tasks at hand, no matter the outcome. Get the site cleaned up and try to answer any questions with enthusiasm.

Once my four-time state-champion team had a problem solution break down in the first minute of an eight-minute presentation. Team members did not quit. They finished everything they could and after the competition they answered questions with smiles. The judges never saw their post-competition heartbreak. I had never been more proud.

TIP #44

Enter and Leave All Sites Smiling

"People only see what they are prepared to see."
–*Ralph Waldo Emerson*

"A fair exterior is a silent recommendation."
–*Publilius Syrus*

"Don't blame the mirror if your face is faulty"
–*Nikolai Gogol*

"By the husk you may guess at the nut."
–*Thomas Fuller*

Tip #45

Do Not Overpractice

"Improvisation is the essence of good talk…put your trust in the inspiration of the moment."
–*Max Beerbohm*

"The individual never asserts himself more than when he forgets himself."
–*André Gide*

"We never do anything well till we cease to think about the manner of doing it."
–*William Hazlitt*

"First learn the meaning of what you say, and then speak."
–*Epictetus*

With slavish over practicing, the performance looses enthusiasm and spontaneity.

One of the biggest problems with creative problem-solving teams at competition is overpracticing. The team should decide how much to practice. Our rule was the "comfort level" rule of practice. If any team member was uncomfortable with the team performance, we did it again. Nobody could deny another practice if a team member requested one.

With slavish overpracticing, I think the performance loses enthusiasm and spontaneity. Another factor to consider is the unexpected. A tightly-memorized performance does not take into account the unexpected and often will not accommodate it well. Some of our best pieces on stage have come from improvisation during practice as well as during the actual competition. Nothing impresses the judges more than a team that overcomes the unexpected during a performance.

It is important that the noncompeting members lend their support and participate.

If, as in some competitions, all team members are not allowed to compete at the same time it is important, just the same, that the noncompeting members lend their support and participate to the greatest legal extent possible.

All teams need to be careful about the rules concerning the solicitation of the audience and the use of handbills. Nonperforming team members can be effective just outside the competition site door, simply talking about the upcoming performance to people as they enter the competition site. In any event, every team member should be given tasks before, during, and after the performance. Prop management, forms, audience preparation, set-up, and take-down are all activities that nonperforming team members may be able to do in some competitions.

TIP #46

Use Every Team Member

"A whole bushel of wheat is made up of single grains."
–*Thomas Fuller*

"United we stand, divided we fall."
–*Benjamin Franklin*

"Union gives strength."
–*Aesop*

"All for one, and one for all."
–*Alexandre Dumas*

Tip #47

Debrief After Every Performance

"We have a need for history in its entirety, not to fall back into it, but to see if we can escape from it."
–*Jose Ortega*

"We can chart our future clearly and wisely only when we know the path which has led to the present."
–*Adlai Stevenson*

"Don't brood on the past, but never forget it either."
–*Thomas Raddall*

One of the most important activities should be the post competition/practice debriefing.

One of the most important coach-initiated activities should be the post-competition or post-practice debriefing: What went right? What went wrong? Where might we improve? What have we seen that we should remember for next year? How did the judges react to our performance? Were our props comparable to those of other teams? Were our sets comparable to those of other teams? Where did we score well? Poorly? Did we enter and leave properly? Did our technology hold up? Did we see any new technology? Was our overall effect satisfactory? Was our performance unique? Did we notice any judging quirks? Did we see any new material uses? What do we need to work on the most? Where were we most successful?

These questions and any others should be written down and displayed at the next team meeting or practice. Pay attention to the team's history if you wish to find the best path in the future.

Reusing materials from previous competitions gives the team a sense of continuity.

Many teams destroy their props after competition. As a coach, look to recover usable pieces or to save certain items in the name of next year's competition.

Ideally a coach should have a garage full of old hardware, electrical motors, paint, and boxes of "we might use this sometime" parts. If you are the head of your school's O.M. program, collect old motors, wiring, switches, dropcloths, sheets, boards, gears, axles, rods, tubes, bicycle parts, and so on.

Moreover, reusing materials from previous competitions gives the team a sense of continuity. I can think of one piece of blue cloth and a podium (or at least parts of it) that have appeared in some form or another at seven national championships!

Tip #48

Save Materials for Next Year

"Men do not realize how great an income thrift is."
–Cicero

"A penny saved is a penny earned."
–Benjamin Franklin

"Waste not, want not."
–Anonymous

Meetings should be planned and they should have a discernible pattern.

TIP #49

Meetings Should Be Planned

"Never put off till tomorrow what you can do today."
–*Thomas Jefferson*

"One cool judgment is worth a thousand hasty counsels. The thing to do is to supply light and not heat."
–*Woodrow Wilson*

Winning coaches will have the appropriate materials available at all practices. Meetings should be planned and, as much as possible, they should have a discernible pattern. If you are going to work on spontaneous problem solving or brainstorming, it should be done at the same time every meeting. Give kids a pattern and they will follow it. Kids need and want structure and are, in fact, comforted by it when under pressure.

In performance problems, the team should list needed items at the end of each meeting and assign team members to find the items before the next meeting.

It is the coach's job to make sure that the materials needed to maintain the pace of creativity are prepared and ready to go at each meeting. If a particular technique is being practiced, the kids should always sit in the same order or take the same position that they will take at competition. They will learn to anticipate what the people on either side of them are going to do.

Some teams are defeated by the site itself, rather than the competition.

Some teams are defeated by the site itself, rather than the competition. Many competitions will give you the particulars of a site if you simply ask before competition. If possible, walk through your performance at the competition site before Murphy's Law comes into effect and something goes wrong. The site corollary of Murphy's Law includes but is not limited to the following.

- Narrow doors, short doors
- Slick, soft, carpeted, or uneven floors
- Pillars
- Air movements that knock over props
- Low ceilings
- Small stages, large stages
- Stairs
- Curtains
- Chair orientation
- Noise levels
- Prestaging area

When you visit the site before competition, look it over and have the team do a visualization exercise. Or do a walk-through to identify any possible problems that the site might present. These activities will also serve to increase the team's comfort level with the site. Pay particular attention to the orientation of the staging area.

TIP #50

The Site Is Part of the Competition

"The three most important things are location, location, location."
–Anonymous

"Your first sight should be the site."
–Richard Safris

"Forewarned is forearmed."
–Anonymous

Tip #51

Field Trips

"They know enough who know how to learn."
–Henry Adams

"Knowledge is power."
–Francis Bacon

"What is the harm in getting knowledge even from a sot, a pot, a fool, a mitten or an old slipper."
–François Rabelais

The team should take a field trip to a lumberyard, hardware store, or junkyard to get ideas for making props and scenery.

Shortly after the theme or style is identified in either a performance or technical problem, the team should take a field trip to a lumberyard, hardware store, or junkyard to get ideas for making props and scenery. The visit also provides the team with a knowledge of the shapes and materials available in these places.

In the past my teams have found visits to plumbing and heating departments of hardware stores to be particularly productive. We discovered Styrofoam®, a light but strong material that can be carved, sanded, or painted. We found that PVC, the pipe material, can be used in a variety of applications. We discovered that nuts and bolts come in a huge variety of sizes and that lightweight, strong aluminum may work when nothing else will.

The advantages of a trip to a live play should be obvious for teams involved in a performance. Watching stage movements, scene changes, staging, and prop use can help a team immeasurably. Most times, with a little work, you can get your team backstage to take a look at the props. It's possible, too, that your team may find a mentor in a local theater group.

Field trips are a welcome break from routine. Yet they should be handled just as a team meeting—with a debriefing and a recording of ideas and concepts.

At the end of the year, we are able to look at the posters and see a road map of where the team had been and where it was probably going.

Set aside walls, ceilings, and floors for competitive teams. Cover them with big sheets of paper containing all kinds of ideas. We did this.

Later In the year, after a project was underway, the idea posters were used less frequently. But we still continued to post goals and successes in the work area. We continued to cross off successes and add details as the year proceeded. We always kept the problem in front of the kids, not off to the side.

At the end of the year, we were able to look at the posters and see a road map of where the team had been and where it was probably going.

Keep in mind that this year's posters can be a springboard for next year's team, when the problem-solving process begins again.

TIP #52

Write Down Every Idea and Post It!

"He writes nothing whose writings are not read."
–*Martial*

"It's like striking a match— sometimes it lights."
–*Neil Simon*

Tools and Training

"Farming looks mighty easy when your plow is a pencil and you're a thousand miles from a cornfield."
–*Dwight D. Eisenhower*

"You can tell a carpenter by his tools."
–*Anonymous*

Teams must have the proper tools to compete successfully.

Teams involved in setbuilding, technical problems, or other types of problems that require construction must have the proper tools to compete successfully. Here are tools that our teams have found to be indispensable.

1. *Hot-glue gun*: A hot-glue gun allows for rapid construction. Low temperature for hot-glue guns is recommended for elementary kids. Hot glue is not a strong glue. Sometimes things will have to be reconstructed with a stronger glue for the performance.

2. *Jigsaw or sabre saw*: The jigsaw is fairly safe for elementary teams, if supervised. Middle-school teams can handle a sabre saw and almost anything can be cut with a sabre saw. A circular saw should be available for high school teams.

3. *Electric drill:* Most teams will need an electric drill. Battery-powered drills are safer since they do not reach the RPM's of plug-in drills. However, battery-powered drills do not drill as quickly.

4. *Dremel tool:* The dremel tool is for prop and set construction. It can be used for detailing, drilling, and carving. It will work particularly well on dense Styrofoam®, allowing props to be made easily with inexpensive materials. Remember, tools can be rented at very little cost.

It is important for teams to establish a pattern of meeting regularly at least once a week during competition preparation.

It is important for teams to establish a pattern of meeting regularly at least once a week during competition preparation. Our teams have met on Sunday afternoons, Tuesday nights, Thursday mornings before school, and Saturday mornings. One year, by working with the school, we were able to arrange a study hall for the team members right before the lunch period. Then we were able to meet during these study halls and through the lunch hour. We usually had a meeting Sunday afternoon, lasting two to four hours, and a meeting of about an hour on Tuesday night. Sundays were working sessions and Tuesdays were typically thinking and visualization sessions until late in the process when they too became work sessions.

A lot of our work was accomplished outside of these meetings. Kids stopped by to work when they had the time; kids took work home; kids took work to school. It is not necessary that every team member attend every meeting. In fact, because kids tend to be very busy, it is often nearly impossible to get them all to each meeting.

TIP #54

Meet on a Regular Schedule

"One of these days is none of those days,"
English proverb

"I recommend you take care of the minutes: For hours will take care of themselves."
–Lord Chesterfield

"What may be done at any time will be done at no time."
–Scottish proverb

TIP #55

Put Down Put-Downs

"If you utter insults you
will also hear them."
–Plautus

"It is often better not
to see an insult."
–Seneca

"An injury is much sooner
forgotten than an insult."
–Lord Chesterfield

**Do not allow criticism ever to
become personal attack.**

The "just kidding" game is a specialty of teenagers
who know the power of words to control and hurt. It is
usually a good game when all of the players are
experts, but sometimes even the experts go too far.
The game involves finding a person's soft spot and
attacking it subtly, waiting for the subtle remark to
register, and then making it socially acceptable by
saying "just kidding."

Over the years, social relationships have been
the greatest problems that I have faced. Demand that
team members respect each other, and do not allow
criticism ever to become personal attack, or your team
is doomed.

Sometimes it is easier for friends to put down
each other down than it is for them to praise each
other. Each coach should—and must—devise
methods to encourage the giving of and acceptance of
compliments.

Help your team by emphasizing completion rather that winning.

Through the years, a major goal of mine has been to teach my teams not to quit in the middle of something. Struggle to the finish, no matter what the eventual outcome. You may lose the competition, but you won't lose your self-respect or the respect of others around you If you do not quit.

Winning teams do not stop their style and skit during competition just because a part of their performance fails. I had a team whose technology broke down in the first part of a three-part problem, destroying any chance they had for winning the competition. But the team didn't quit. It finished in fourth place in a 20-team division, despite its early breakdown. Team members knew they couldn't win, but they finished the competition anyway.

Help your team by emphasizing completion rather than winning. If the team completes the competition and does its best, it has succeeded.

TIP #56

Never Quit Trying!

"The secret of success is constancy to purpose."
–Benjamin Disraeli

"You always pass failure on the way to success."
–Mickey Rooney

"'Tis a lesson you should heed, try, try again. If at first you don't succeed, try, try again."
–William E. Hickson

Develop a Team Philosophy

"Philosophy can be defined as the art of asking the right questions."
–Abraham Joshua Heschel

"What is good for the hive is good for the bee."
–Marcus Aurelius

"Teach me to live without uncertainty and yet without being paralyzed by hesitation, is perhaps the chief thing philosophy can still do."
–Bertrand Russell

Winning teams will develop a group philosophy.

Winning teams will develop a group philosophy, or a sort of "guidebook" for their dealings with each other and for their method of attacking the problem. Our team philosophy included the following.

1. Never quit!
2. Never accept the first solution.
3. Elaborate, elaborate, elaborate.
4. Work never divides evenly.
5. Respect is the foundation.
6. Never criticize until you can offer a better solution or you have identified a specific reason for your criticism.
7. Simplify technology as much as possible without sacrificing creativity.
8. Enter smiling.
9. Leave smiling.

What things are important to your team? Set down the guideposts to success and team happiness. Emphasize that all goals and methods are simply temporary and can be adjusted should a better method or goal come along. Encourage team discussions about what members expect from each other and from the team as a whole. Every idea that you can get out in the open is one less problem waiting to jump out and grab you.

Working together can generate synergies never thought of individually.

If nothing seems to generate an idea that the team can agree upon, just start with everybody developing parallel ideas. Working together and talking out loud as the various ideas are explored can generate synergies never thought of individually. As some ideas fall by the wayside, others will grow stronger until eventually the winning idea will present itself. A unified whole may come out of diverse ideas.

I have had success with brainstorming the title of the problem or important words in the instructions as a starting point for the problem solution. Actually, that is usually our first brainstorming session with each new problem. Often a matrix (see pages 79–82) can help to identify the best idea as well as team strengths and weaknesses.

TIP #58

If Necessary, Just Start

"A hard beginning maketh a good ending."
—*Proverb*

"In creating, the only hard thing is to begin."
—*James Russell Lowell*

"A journey of a thousand miles must begin with a single step."
—*Lao-tzu*

"Begin at the beginning … and go on till you come to the end: then stop."
—*Lewis Carroll*

TIP #59

Have High Aspirations

"For all sad words of tongue and pen, the saddest are these: It might have been."
–*John Greenleaf Whittier*

"The significance of a man is not in what he attains but rather in what he longs to attain."
–*Kahlil Gibran*

"Winning isn't everything, but wanting to win is."
–*Vince Lombardi*

Mediocre goals generate mediocre performances.

One of the most difficult tasks for a problem-solving coach is to teach the team to set high but realistically attainable goals. If the goals are not set high enough, the results will reflect it. Mediocre goals generate mediocre performances. Yet if goals are set too high, frustration and panic will result.

Perhaps the most important part of goal setting is the realization that goals must be, by their very nature, changeable. The final goals should be performance-oriented—general in tone but specific in detail. An example would be: "Our goal is to put ourselves in the position to win. We will do this by elaboration and detail in our solution to this problem. In particular, we will make better costumes than we have in the past."

Goals should set pathways to success. The general goal must address recurring problems that the team has had in the past in order to correct these deficiencies. Underlying the general goal are performance goals, stated in terms of who, what, when, and how. For example, "By October 15, Bill will have completed the rough draft of the script."

All goals should be written on large pieces of paper and posted on the walls of the work area, if possible. Each goal should be crossed off as it is accomplished. This gives the team a sense of progress and a feeling of success.

Coaches must be willing to fail in front of their teams if they expect their teams to fail in front of them.

If you respect your team members and at the same time earn their respect by your actions, half the battle will be won.

Coaches must be willing to fail in front of their teams if they expect their teams to fail in front of them. Get beat at chess, lose at video games, or let team members have the last word when they have beaten you in a wordplay or an argument. If you do something stupid, admit it. Teenagers, although they will not usually admit it, feel stupid at least once a day and they will understand what you are feeling.

To be a good coach, you must share the feelings of your team. When something the team has worked on for weeks fails, feel what the team is feeling. Accept team members as equals and lead them with experience, instead of beating them up with it, and you will be a solid team.

TIP #60

Team Discipline

"It is better to bind your children to you by a feeling of respect, and by gentleness, than by fear."
–*Terrence*

"It is not enough to be busy... the question is: What are we busy about?"
–*Henry David Thoreau*

"I'm a great believer in luck, and I find the harder I work the more I have of it."
–*Thomas Jefferson*

Problem Solving Is a Process

"To lose is to learn."
–Anonymous

"What is defeat? Nothing but education, nothing but the first step toward something better."
–Wendell Phillips

"A good problem statement often includes (a) what is known; (b) what is unknown; and (c) what is sought."
–Edward Hodnett

"To be what we are, and to become what we are capable of becoming, is the only end of life."
–Robert Louis Stevenson

Goals must be constantly redirected and fine-tuned.

Understand that the problem-solving process is never actually done. Every new solution opens up new horizons and new pitfalls. The problem-solving team must never rest on its laurels because pitfalls are usually lurking just out of sight. Every leap of progress opens up new risks. Team members must constantly keep their eyes open for a seemingly solid idea that is resting on a bed of quicksand.

We constantly revised and changed our solutions as new avenues opened up. Preconception must be avoided. Goals must be constantly redirected and fine-tuned. Like driving down Interstate 80, you are almost certain to hit a construction zone or a detour somewhere. Every detour is a chance to see some new part of the country and to learn from it. Every "construction zone" exposes the team to different ways of doing things.

Genius only has value if it is applied.

What is genius? Is it the ability to sew at age ten, or is it the ability to hit a nail on the head at age nine? Does it involve being able to work with other kids and understand their needs? Coaches must approach their teams with the idea that every kid is a genius. It becomes the task of the team to let the genius in each child bloom.

"Stupid is as stupid does," or so Forrest Gump would have us believe. The corollary to this theory is "genius is as genius does." Genius only has value if it is applied. Successful teams locate the genius hidden in each member and utilize it. As a coach, you must do your best to find and use the genius in each child.

Coaches must remember that in many problem-solving contests, skill with a hammer is every bit as valuable as knowledge of electrical circuits. Andy Warhol told us that everyone is famous for 15 minutes. As a coach, if you can find that time slot for each of your kids, you will have a successful problem-solving solution.

Coaches must also realize that genius often carries with it a penalty in unusual or unpredictable behavior. Sometimes unusual behaviors are, in fact, the expression of genius. If you want genius, you must go with the flow and let things work themselves out.

TIP #62

Know the Definition of Genius

"Towering genius disdains a beaten path; it seeks regions hitherto unexplored."
–*Abraham Lincoln*

"Genius, in truth, means little more than the faculty of perceiving in an unhabitual way."
–*William James*

"The difference between genius and stupidity is that genius has its limits."
–*Anonymous*

"Genius is 1 percent inspiration and 99 percent perspiration"
–*Thomas Edison*

TIP #63

Use History as a Springboard to Success

"The problems of victory are more agreeable than those of defeat, but they are no less difficult."
-Winston Churchill

"Lose as if you like it; win as if you were used to it."
–Tommy Hitchcock

"Know thyself."
–Sophocles

A new team should inventory the team skills it possesses.

If a team does not know its own strengths and weaknesses, it will have difficulty building a problem solution. A first-year team will have less to go on than more experienced teams. A new team should inventory the skills it possesses. In some cases, kids will tell you what they are good at, though most kids are reluctant to toot their own horns.

In some cases you will be able to find out what your team members' skills are through observation. In other cases, you may discover that skills will only blossom during events.

Sometimes societal pressures will divide a team along gender lines. In other words, the girls will make the costumes and do the artwork and music, while the boys will build the sets or do the technological work. Watch for this division and stop it if you can.

I particularly remember the first year of a team when the boys said, "You girls write the script and we'll make the vehicle." When all was said and done, the girls had made significant inroads on making the vehicle and the boys ended up writing the script. Use skills wherever they lie.

Success breeds success.

Winning teams will always strike while the iron is hot.

For coaches this means

1. Getting in the car during the middle of the Super Bowl and going for materials.
2. Always being prepared for meetings.
3. Solving social problems early.
4. Letting some meetings run much longer than planned.
5. Letting kids work on their own outside of the meetings.

For the team this means

1. Writing down good ideas whenever they occur.
2. Staying late at meetings if things are really rolling.
3. Bringing materials to meetings, if requested.
4. If other things prevent you from attending meetings, working when you have the time.
5. Staying focused when things are going well.

For parents this means

1. Getting the kids to meetings.
2. Listening to what your child has to say and being a sounding board for his or her ideas.

Success breeds success. When the team is running well, let it run.

TIP #64

Strike While the Iron Is Hot

"If you think you can win, you can win. Faith is necessary to victories."
–Publilius Syrus

"Who seeks and will not take when once tis offer'd shall never find it more."
–William Shakespeare

"We must take the current when it serves or lose our ventures."
–William Shakespeare

TIP #65

Have No Regrets

"Make it a rule of life never to regret and never look back. Regret is an appalling waste of energy; you can't build on it, it's good only for wallowing in."
–Katharine Mansfield

"Let us not burden our remembrances with a heaviness that is gone."
–William Shakespeare

"There is nothing wrong with making mistakes, just don't respond with encores."
–Anonymous

The only truly important errors are errors of omission.

When a team has created the best solution possible given its experience and skills, that team should never have any serious regrets. Emphasize, however, that the only truly important errors are errors of omission, because errors of omission reflect a lack of preparation and thought.

Coaches must approach failure in a businesslike, controlled manner. It's up to you, coach. Will your team members think of themselves as victims unable to control their own fate or as experienced problem-solvers with knowledge of how to do a better job the next time?

Solutions do not have to be complex and intricately drawn to be creative.

In the fourteenth century, Occam (Okham) gave us an important clue to problem-solving. He recognized that there is a beauty inherent in simple solutions to difficult, complex problems. Judges will appreciatively score any solution that makes them say, "Why didn't I think of that?!"

It should be noted that solutions do not have to be complex and intricately drawn to be creative. In fact, some of the most creative solutions to problems are indeed the simplest.

Although simplicity is recommended, deal with it carefully. Sometimes there is a danger of oversimplifying a complex problem. If we oversimplify, we may generalize an answer that does not specifically meet the needs of the problem. The key is to reduce variables. Attempt to reduce the paths that could result from any action to the point that all of the paths have acceptable outcomes for the problem solution.

TIP #66

Shave Your Performance with Occam's Razor

"Everything should be made as simple as possible but not simpler."
–Albert Einstein

"Entia non sunt multiplicanda praeter necessitatem."
(Entities should not be multiplied unnecessarily.)*
–William of Ockham

*Don't make it any more complicated than it is.

TIP #67

Admit Failure but Do Not Accept It

"There are defeats more triumphant than victories.
–*Montaigne*

"We are all failures,
at least the best of us are."
–*J. M. Barrie*

"Studious to please,
yet not ashamed to fail."
–*Samuel Johnson*

Team members must be willing to fail.

In order for teams to be successful, the team members must be willing to fail. They must take risks as they stretch their resources to solve difficult problems. They must be willing to admit that they have failed at a task and ask for help—from their teammates, from books, from mentors, from whatever the best source seems to be in the situation.

Failure is but one part of the process. Teams must learn to work through the failure and not quit. For particularly bright team members, any failure may be a traumatic event. In fact, they may never have failed before at anything they have tried. Coaches must understand just how difficult failure is for these kids.

Good teams hate failure with a passion, but they recognize it as part of the process and just one more step on the path to success.

The best teams tend to be self-selected.

Team selection usually falls into three categories. In the self-selection process the team finds itself; in directed selection the teams are arranged by a teacher or school authority; and in competitive selection the team members are selected based on some set of criteria.

It has been my experience that the best teams tend to be self-selected. I believe the very best teams occur when a few highly motivated individuals recruit skilled, compatible individuals to be on the team. For example, members may discover that they have no one with electrical knowledge and the problem calls for skills in this area. The team may then go out and find a compatible teammate with the necessary skills.

Experienced teams may find themselves in this position when one or more team members choose not to participate in competition for the next year. Good teams will select new members on the basis of compatibility and need rather than on friendship. The coach may have to help the team see the difference between compatibility and friendship.

I believe that teams should be kept together from year to year if they choose to stay together. A key to success in competition is to get the team to the point where teammates know each other so well that they learn to anticipate each other's needs and responses.

TIP #69

Sell the Sizzle

"It is easy to be beautiful;
it is difficult to appear so."
–Frank O'Hara

"Your first appearance," he said to
me, "is the gauge by which you
will be measured."
–Jean Jacques Rousseau

"To establish oneself in the world,
one has to do all one can to
appear established."
–François de La Rochefoucauld

**The sizzle grabs the attention of the judges
and the quality wins you the points.**

Winning teams will recognize that quality is important, but just as important is the concept of "selling the sizzle." This old sales term means that quality will pay in the long run, but you must get them "to buy" before they will notice the quality. The sizzle grabs the attention of the judges, and the quality wins the points.

If you do not grab the judges' attention at the beginning of the skit and also at various times during the skit when you are making your points, you will not score well. You must get the judges' attention early and build to miniclimaxes to keep their attention level at a maximum during the entire performance. Remember, grabbing the judges' attention begins before the performance. Your professional but friendly attitude during precompetition may positively affect later results. Your attitude toward the judges should be, "We are in this together and we're going to enjoy it."

Be careful not to place all of your best or biggest moments at the beginning of your performance. You do not want your performance to go downhill from the beginning to the end.

Analyze every word of the problem.

TIP #70

Reading the Problem

"Knowledge is of two kinds. We know a subject ourselves, or we know where we can find information upon it."
–*Samuel Johnson*

"I find that a great part of the information I have was acquired by looking up something and finding something else on the way."
–*Franklin P. Adams*

"Books must be read as deliberately as they are written."
–*Henry David Thoreau*

As soon as the coach receives a copy of the problem, the team should see it. If the next year's problems are available, read and discuss them. Here are some things to do.

1. Read the problem aloud at the first meeting. Discuss what you've read and then have a team member read the problem aloud. If there is a summary of the problem, read it aloud and discuss it at length.

2. Analyze every word of the problem. Analyzing includes looking up the definition of each verb and noun, even if you think you know the meanings.

3. Read the scoring description aloud and discuss every area that is to be scored. Determine whether the problem is largely objective or subjective in nature.

4. Brainstorm all important words in the problem description. Look for parallel situations which may make good themes. Try synonyms for words in the problem description to get different slants on the problem. For example, "hybrid relays" becomes "corn races," which becomes "corn people," which becomes a theme in which corn takes over the world and writes revisionist history.

Final Thoughts

Somewhere at this moment a creative problem-solving team is sitting around a kitchen table. Members of that team will solve one of the great problems facing our world. It may be *your* kitchen table at which they are sitting.

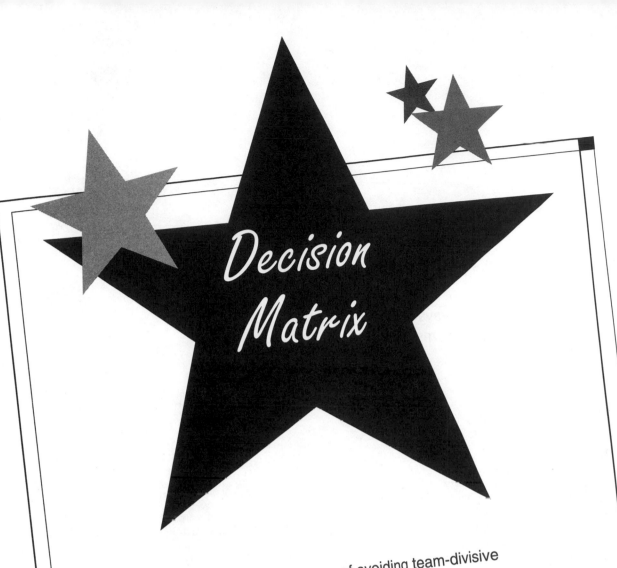

Decision Matrix

Matrix decision making is a way of avoiding team-divisive votes. A simple example follows.

A problem has come up in the construction of a project. A washer needs to be firmly fastened to a bolt. One of the girls wants to weld the washer in place, another wants to use epoxy putty, and a third wants to use contact cement. A decision needs to be made, but the coach wishes to avoid a vote, so a matrix is set up (see pages 80–82).

The team takes the following steps.

1. First the team must define the problem.
    The problem: How can the team firmly attach a washer to a bolt?

2. The team discusses possible ways of attaching the washer to the bolt and arrives at the following possible methods of attachment.

    • Welding

    • Contact cement

    • Epoxy putty

    • White glue

3. The team then discusses what the limiting factors are on their ability to use these methods and they arrive at the following limiting factors.

    • Do we have the skills?

    • Do we have the supplies?

    • Will it be strong enough?

    • How expensive will it be?

    • Do we have the time to do it?

    • Do we have the tools to do it?

4. Then they put these methods and limitations in a matrix. Sample matrix is on the next page.

Each solution is discussed and ranked from 1 to 10 based on the criteria listed beneath the matrix.

1 = worst   10 = best

							Total Rank
Welding	1	1	10	5	5	1	23
Contact cement	10	8	1	10	10	10	49
White glue	10	10	1	10	10	10	51
Epoxy putty	10	8	10	9	10	10	57

1. Do we have the skills?
2. Do we have the supplies?
3. Will it be strong enough?
4. How expensive will it be?
5. Do we have the time to do it?
6. Do we have the tools to do it?

Epoxy gets the nod, and it has been selected by the matrix, not by a divisive vote.

Some coaches may want to determine each individual rating by discussion. Others may wish to give each team member a matrix and then average the score for each position before putting it on the final matrix. Some matrix users will assign values to criteria based on importance. The scores are then multiplied by that value before being entered in the matrix.

For example, in the matrix above, if the team ranked the criteria and decided that #3 was the most important and #5 was the least important, we might then multiply all of the scores above the #3 limitation by 10 and all of the scores above the #5 by 1, or some variation on this theme, before totaling the scores. This usually spreads the final scores a little more and will probably lead to a more accurate decision than a nonweighted matrix.

An example of a weighted matrix follows on page 82.

Weighted Matrix

Weight	10	4	8	1	6	2	Total
Welding	10	4	80	5	30	2	131
Contact cement	100	32	8	10	60	20	230
White glue	100	40	8	10	60	20	238
Epoxy putty	100	32	80	9	60	20	301

1. Do we have the skills?

2. Do we have the supplies?

3. Will it be strong enough?

4. How expensive will it be?

5. Do we have the time to do it?

6. Do we have the tools to do it?

Ranking of Importance

Most important

- Do we have the skills?   Weight :10

- Do we have the supplies?   Weight: 8

- Will it be strong enough?   Weight: 6

- How expensive will it be?   Weight: 4

- Do we have the time to do it?   Weight: 2

- Do we have the tools to do it?   Weight: 1

The individual scores from the matrix on the previous page were multiplied by the weight factors to produce the numbers on the sample matrix. For example, at the intersection of "Welding" and "Do we have the skills?" the original number was 1, which in this matrix was multiplied by the weighting of 10 to get the weighted result of 10.

In this matrix the final results are the same as in the unweighted matrix. But in most cases, weighting will lead to different and probably more acceptable results, particularly if one or two limitations are very important factors in the solution.

Materials and Supplies

This section contains information about materials and supplies. Sometimes the quest for a creative solution to a problem becomes a scavenger hunt of gigantic proportions. This scavenger hunt may very well make the difference between success and failure. Thus on the following pages I have listed several "tried and true" sources of materials and supplies and a few creative uses that your team may not have considered. A good creative problem-solving team will establish its own sources of materials and supplies and never forget them. Team members will be watching constantly for new items, uses, and sources that may be utilized at some other time.

Plastic Foam (Styrofoam®)

Plastic foam is my material of choice for elementary- and middle-school children because it is easy to use. This is not to say that plastic foam should be avoided by high school students, because—at any age—it can be easily cut with common hand tools, even kitchen utensils. It is also light and can be easily moved around, so it becomes a natural choice for younger children.

There are several other reasons why I recommend plastic foam.

- It can be shaped with a file or other utensils and sanded easily.

- It can be easily painted with latex paint.

- It can be coated with plaster, plastic wood, or saw dust and glue to make a smooth surface.

- It can be cut using a jigsaw or other common hand tools.

- It is relatively cheap when compared with plywood or cloth, and only requires a lightweight support system to make it stand up.

- You can glue, screw, or nail it together or to other props.

- Last, but not least, it is easily obtainable.

Different sizes, thicknesses, shapes, and densities of plastic foam are carried by most lumberyards and many hobby stores. The cost of plastic foam is usually determined predominantly by its density—the more dense the product, the greater its strength and the higher the cost. If you don't wish to purchase plastic foam, recycle some. Motorcycle shops, appliance stores, electronic stores, home construction sites, among other places, are usually excellent sources for pieces of plastic foam.

Environmental concerns about plastic foam may bother many teachers, parents, and children. If you are concerned, I would invite you to look up the latest research comparing plastic foam with, for example, cardboard as an environmental hazard. Perhaps you'll pledge to use only previously-used plastic foam (recycled from some other use) as a solution you can live with.

Lumber, Plywood, and Balsa Wood

Almost every creative problem-solving project involving a performance ends up with some plywood in it somewhere. Lumber can be purchased at your local lumberyard, but that often becomes very expensive very quickly. If you must purchase lumber, I suggest the following alternatives to reduce the cost:

- Use waferboard or masonite.

- Use 1" x 2" or 2" x 2" furring strip lumber instead of 2" x 4" or higher-grade 1" x 2"s or 2" x 2"s pieces. The use of smaller lumber will reduce not only the cost but also the weight of the project.

- Ask about scrap lumber from custom cutting.

- Ask about badly warped, discolored, or split pieces.

- Buy precut utility studs instead of standard 8' pieces.

- Always buy the thinnest, cheapest grade of plywood that will work in your application.

- Most large towns have salvage yards that are sources of all types and sizes of used lumber at very reasonable prices compared with the cost of new lumber. Look in your Yellow Pages for these sources.

- Balsa wood can be found at hobby stores and has many applications in creative projects. It is light and strong and can be easily shaped and glued.

- Balsa wood can be obtained in different grades directly from the manufacturer. Contact Sig Manufacturing of Montezuma, Iowa, for a price list of different sizes and grades of balsa wood.

- Before you buy any lumber, check your Sunday paper. Most of the lumber that you need will be on sale somewhere local.

If you do not wish to buy lumber, try these other sources. You will rarely be turned down if the lumber you ask for is indeed scrap lumber.

- Check home construction sites. Talk to the framing carpenters and ask them to save usable pieces for you. In most cases, they will be glad to let you have the scraps. You may even discover a mentor.

- Locally owned lumberyards sometimes will save you their scraps from custom-cutting at no cost if you ask them to help you out.

- Run an ad in the local shopping flier or small newspaper asking for the community's help in locating materials of all types.

- Ask a family member or friend who does woodworking for some scraps.

- Shipping and manufacturing firms often will have broken crates and pallets that they will give you at no cost.

- Local millwork or cabinetry firms may have lumber scraps of different types and sizes. This lumber is more likely to be hardwood, which is heavier but much stronger and more durable than pine or fir.

Fome-cor®

Fome-cor® is composed of a thin sheet of plastic foam with cardboard or paper on each side of it. Its smooth surface, lightness, and strength make it an excellent medium for small props, backdrops, and artwork. Unfortunately, new Fome-cor® is expensive. You can make your own by gluing butcher paper or thin cardboard on both sides of plastic foam sheets from the lumberyard. Here are some other possibilities.

- Sometimes Fome-cor® scraps are available from advertising agencies (they often use it in presentations).

- Architectural firms may offer scraps of Fome-cor® left over from the backings on drawings.

- Art galleries may have some scrap Fome-cor® available from their packing of art objects and pictures.

- Fome-cor® can be created by spraying nonexpanding insulation foam on a sheet of thin cardboard and then sandwiching another piece of cardboard on top of the foam before the foam dries.

Aluminum

Often ignored in construction projects, aluminum has great strength, is relatively easy to cut and shape, is lightweight, and is easily obtainable. It is the material of choice when great strength with little weight is desired.

- Aluminum can be purchased at most lumberyards and aluminum fabricating firms.

- Scrap can be purchased fairly cheaply from most building salvage yards.

- Aluminum can be salvaged from old windows and storm doors.

- The high school or middle school industrial arts teacher may have what you need.

Cardboard

- Inquire at appliance stores for large pieces of heavy cardboard. Refrigerator cartons are usually quite heavy and strong.

- Watch home construction sites. Some of the best cardboard comes wrapped around whirlpool bathtubs and spas. New houses also usually have new appliances, which come in cardboard boxes.

- Ask at spa stores for cardboard.

- Specialty cardboard can often be found at art stores.

- Teachers can often obtain small sheets of cardboard or posterboard at minimal cost.

Paint and Paintbrushes

- Most latex paints can be mixed with each other easily and effectively to create new colors. Do not attempt to mix oil-based and latex paint together.

- Avoid the use of spray paint, if you can, because it is expensive. If you must use it, you may be able to reduce the expense by first brushing on a thin coat of latex paint.

- Ask at the paint store, lumberyard, or hardware store to see if they have any mismatched, odd lot, or incorrectly mixed paint that they would sell to you.

- Always buy the cheapest paint available, since it doesn't have to last long.

- Try food coloring to tint small amounts of paint for detail work.

- Hot gelatin will set colors nicely in many fabrics and is much cheaper than dye. It will also work to color latex paint.

- Easter egg coloring can be used to color many things.

- Try tempera paint mixed with white latex paint to create a better finish than regular tempera.

- Avoid straight tempera, if possible, because it cracks easily on props and sometimes peels or breaks off of backdrops.

- Undercoat all cloth or plywood with latex before trying to draw or paint on those materials.

- Always save your mixes to make repairs. Baby jars, racquetball cans, and even plastic bags are handy containers.

- Most hardware stores sell disposable paintbrushes that are inexpensive and good for several applications.

- Paintbrushes can be stored in the freezer in a plastic bag instead of cleaning them each time.

Cloth and Cloth Substitutes

If you can afford the expense, cloth on frames is vastly superior to cardboard for use as backdrops. Cloth is more durable, flexible, easier to use, and better-looking than painted cardboard.

- Check the remnant table at the fabric goods store and find out if your school might receive a discount.

- Purchase old sheets at garage sales, or look in the bottom of your linen closet.

- Consider using old canvas or plastic dropcloths.

- Sew or glue small pieces of cloth together to get a desired size.

- Hot glue works quite well on cloth. Iron it after sewing or gluing to smooth it out.

- Consider using paper instead of cloth. Paper with latex paint on it is quite durable.

- Tissue paper, when stretched and painted with dope (a special paint) or thinned latex will become quite durable after several coats. Make repairs on the backside or reinforce with strips of duct tape.

Electrical Supplies

- Electricity is both a powerful friend and a dangerous enemy. Even 12 volts can give a meaningful shock to a child. Watch carefully when working with electricity and make sure that the batteries are never cut open and that the household current is not used in a dangerous way.

- Hardware stores and lumberyards usually sell switches and wiring.

- Hobby stores carry small lights, sockets, and motors as well as miniature structural parts that can be quite useful.

- Electronic stores will usually have many things that you didn't even know existed. Many good ideas may be generated by standing and looking at the variety of things in an electronics store.

- Electrical salvage yards should have cheap parts.

- Take apart nonfunctioning toys and appliances to get usable motors and other parts.

- Never take apart old TV sets or other electronic items that generate high voltage and utilize large capacitors.

- Take apart old toys to get battery cases or use different sizes of PVC pipe to make your own cases for different sizes of batteries.

- New houses usually have lots of pieces of scrap wire laying around after the electricians have finished wiring.

- See the catalogs listed on page 91.

Duct Tape

- Use it to reinforce.

- Use it to make costumes.

- Use it rolled up to serve as a very strong rope.

- Use it to hold parts together while they are being nailed or glued.

- Use it to reinforce seams on cardboard sets.

- Do not be without it! It is perhaps the most versatile of materials.

Catalogs

Every creative problem-solving team should have access to the following catalogs.

Herbach and Rademan
18 Canal Street
P.O. Box 122
Bristol, PA 19007–1233
Phone: (215) 788–5583
Fax: (215) 788–9577

Archie McPhee
Box 30852
Seattle, WA 98103
Phone: (206) 782–2344
Fax: (206) 782–9413

Edmund Scientific
101 East Gloucester Pike
Barrington Pike, NJ 08007–1380
Phone: (609) 573–6879
Fax: (609) 573–6295

American Science Surplus
601 Linden Place
Evanston, IL 60202
Phone: (708) 475–8440
Fax: (708) 864–1589

Any team that cannot find what it needs in these catalogs should revise its outlook on creative problem-solving. In fact, most teams will find things they never even knew they needed from reading these catalogs.

Notes

Notes

Notes

Notes

Notes